A Cat's Life

My ☆ Own Story

P Peter Pauper Press, Inc.
White Plains, New York

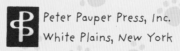

By Roni Schraeder

Illustrated and designed by
Kerren Barbas

Printed on acid-free paper
Illustrations copyright © 1999
Kerren Barbas
Text copyright © 1999
Peter Pauper Press, Inc.
202 Mamaroneck Avenue
White Plains, NY 10601
ISBN 0-88088-644-7
Printed in China
10 9 8 7

Visit us at www.peterpauper.com

Contents

It has been the providence of Nature
to give this creature nine lives.

Pilpay

A cat is a special member of the family.
Each day brings memories to last a lifetime.
Here is a place to keep them.

Welcome Home

I arrived

My family

My first address

Here's what my home looked like when I arrived

place picture here

What's in a Name?

My name

My name was chosen by

My name was chosen because

I was almost called

Nicknames

Sometimes I'm called

Signs of the Time

Here's what the world looked like when I arrived

The U.S. President

The film that won the Academy Award® for best picture

The cost of cat food

Newspaper headlines

place a newspaper clipping here

Cat Preferences

My favorite place to sleep

My favorite place to sit

My favorite game

My favorite food

Cattitude

*Cats possess so many of the same
qualities of some people...
that it's often hard to tell
the people and the cats apart.*

P. J. O'Rourke
Modern Manners

I am very picky

I keep to myself

I love on my own terms

Cat "Tails"

Here are some stories about me

I can be very funny

I look really cute

The biggest mess I ever made

One time I was a hero

Cats...
never strike a pose that isn't photogenic.
Lillian Jackson Braun

Picture Pages

Get a Camera for these poses!

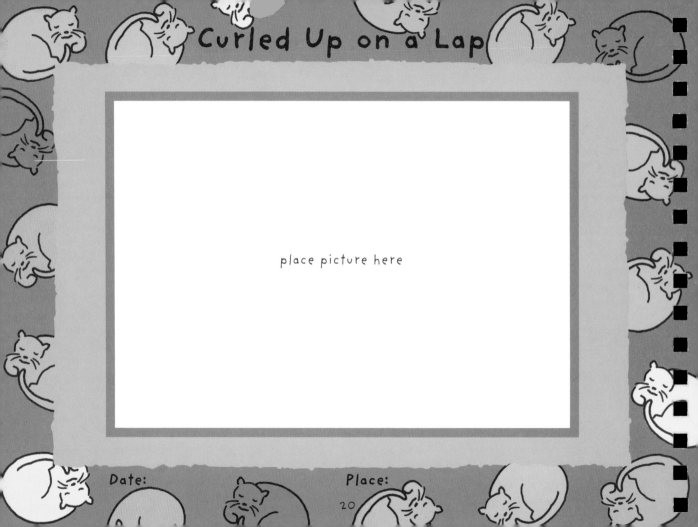

place picture here

Date:

Place:

20

Hide & Seek

place picture here

Date:

Place:

21

Lazy Cat

place picture here

Date: Place:

Curious Cat

place picture here

Date: Place:

place picture here

Date:

Place:

Smart Cat

place picture here

Date: Place:

Reading the Newspaper

place picture here

Date: Place:

Sleepy Cat

place picture here

Date: Place:

Cat In the Hat

place picture here

Date: Place:

28

place picture here

Date:

Place:

Sunny Day

place picture here

Date: Place:

Fat Cat

place picture here

Date: Place:

Sitting On the TV

place picture here

Date:

Place:

Who's That In the Mirror?

place picture here

Date: Place:

Halloween Cat

place picture here

Date: Place:

Thanksgiving Cat

place picture here

Date: Place:

Holiday Cat

place picture here

Date: Place:

New Year's Cat

place picture here

Date:

Place:

Keepsakes

Fur Ball

Pet Tags

Piece of Favorite String

Veterinarian

Name

Telephone Number

Address

Vet Visits

Kittens—8 weeks to 1 year

Date

8 weeks	•First vaccination shot (FVRCP)
12 weeks	•Feline leukemia shot (FeLV) (only if pretest is negative) •A second (FeLV) shot 2-3 weeks later •Second vaccination shot (FVRCP)
4 months	•Rabies & third vaccination shot (FVRCP)

Adult cats—over 1 year

FVRCP—yearly	•Cats 13 weeks or older that have not been vaccinated should have an initial vaccine, then a booster in 2-4 weeks.
FeLV—yearly	•Cats not previously vaccinated need the 2 injection series (only if pretest is negative)
Rabies—yearly	•depending on vaccine

Vet Visits

Annual Check-ups	Date

Cat Descriptives

affectionate
alley cat
aloof
amazing
arch
attitude
best friend
black
breed
calico
camouflage
can-opener
catnip
catnap
character
cheetah

claws
comfort
content
coy
cozy
curious
delicate
demanding
devilish
distinguished
docile
drop
eccentric
embarrassed
energetic
extrovert
fat

feast
floppy
fluffy
frisky
fur balls
fuzzy
goddess
hiding
high strung
intelligent
intense
jealous
klutz
lap
lazy
lion
longhair

Cat Descriptives

lucky
meow
mouse
nap
neat
nervous
newspaper
nibble
noble
out and about
outgoing
pampered
paws
pedigree
perfect
perfumed
Persian

playful
plush
pose
pounce
predator
pretty
purr
ragdoll
rare
regal
roll
rub
scratch
shorthaired
shy
Siamese
sleepy

stretch
string
swat
tabby
tapping
territorial
tiger
tom cat
toys
traveler
treats
tuna
twitchy-nose
vulnerable
whiner
whiskers
wild cat

Notes

Notes

Notes

Notes

The End